The **JOURNEY** To Reach *My* *Calling*

By Jordan Windmon

Copywrite April 2019 ©

By Author Jordan Windmon

All rights reserved. All entries are original writings from the author and may not be reused as original content by another individual.

Publication of Writers4Christ, LLC ™ May 2019

Dedication

I dedicate this book to my mother, Janice Windmon. She was known by the name Krikit. I thank God for all that He empowered you to say and do to raise me and your sons. You taught us to love God and live only for Him. I'm so thankful for everything you've done for us. I'm grateful that you're now in peace at God's throne. I ask that you keep watching over me and the boys. I pray when our time comes you'll see us again. I love and miss you so much momma!

My New Day Has Begun

My life is full of stress and pain so I talk to the Holy Spirit

I know He's talking back but for some reason I just can't hear it

With the pain me and my brothers are going through because of the woman we lost

I'll do anything to hear what He's saying at just about any cost

Momma taught us that the Holy Spirit can break us free from anything

I think it's much easier if we praise Him with our voice and come out and sing

Many people do this, we do crazy things but when we need something we go to Christ

But since we only want something and don't give to him we're just many mumbling mice

With the stuff I'm going through I need a new beginning

That means I have to stop what I'm doing because in His eyes all that is, is sinning

I'm not going to say it's going to be easy because that's a lie

But I'm going to keep praying and telling myself you have to try

Like momma said the Holy Spirit brings up the sun

So I'm going to lift my hands and say thank You Lord

<u>My New Day Has Begun</u>!

See Me Through

What am I supposed to do in a world like this?

It drives me so crazy I use to cut my wrist;

Lord with all the mistakes I've made how can you still love me?

With all the wrong doings I've done the good side is so hard to see.

Through you I know anything can happen;

But with this pain piece by piece my heart keeps snappin'

What I need to know is why I can't hear you talking?

I know if I don't get your message soon the enemy will just keep stalking.

When I'm in church sometimes I can feel you;

Why you won't stay I really have no clue.

Because of the enemy my heart is full of madness and wrong;

That makes me want to go back to my room and sing another sad song.

Lord you have to tell me what I can do to make this right;

Momma singing to me about you is the only thing I have in sight.

Sadly I'm an emotional wreck and don't know what to do;

But because of the GREAT Lord I know You are you will

<u>See Me Through</u>.

No Longer

What did I do to deserve something like this?

Because of the enemy my life is constantly getting dissed.

I know I've made many mistakes and done several things wrong;

But devil you need to back off I've feared you too long!

In the past you've made me very weak;

Now the healing of the Holy Spirit is all I seek.

You've taken many things from me and my mom is one;

So I'm going to find my way back to God's All Mighty Son.

I'm praying to God to make me much stronger;

Because devil, I refuse to fear you any longer!

You will not mess with me and my family anymore;

I'm sick of you making our hearts so very sore.

From now on, from you our hearts and souls are sealed;

We rebuke you, and by HIS stripes we are healed.

Momma left us with the Word of God in our hearts forever;

Thanks momma, it's made us more clever.

Over the years God has made us much stronger;

So devil step back! You will mess with us <u>No Longer</u>!

So Very Close

Devil what makes you think you can take over my life?

No matter what I'm going to find my way back to Christ.

You've brought so many storms to my heart and mind;

But the storm is over now there's only a small mountain I need to climb.

I can't give up now, my path is almost clear;

So thanks to God there are only a few things I fear.

If it wasn't for Him by now I probably would've quit;

Thank you Lord! Without you I never would've made it.

I don't see how He does it, but He always sees the best in me;

There's no doubt I'll get my breakthrough and it will set me free.

When I'm in church sometimes I can feel Your powerful hand upon my heart;

Without that power, by now the devil would've torn me apart.

I refuse to let this beat me so I'm going to fight harder than most;

With this motivation I can tell my breakthrough is So Very Close!

More Than I Can Bare

Lately it feels like a lot of weights been put on my shoulders;

I know it's because of the enemy that my heart feels colder.

Why does it seem like my anger and sensitivity are getting worse;

If it is, I pray I'm not under a demonic curse.

Why is it my soul that the enemy wants to destroy?

He plays with it every day like it's a toy.

Last time I checked I said, "devil I'm not going to fear you;"

I don't break my word, that's something I won't do.

Right now there's so much pain I'm going through;

It's coming so fast I don't know what to do.

I know God is with me, and I'm wrapped in His arms;

With His power and protection there's no way I can get harmed.

Because I want to get back with God, I'll be one of the main one the devil tries to scare;

But no matter what God will never give me <u>More Than I Can Bare</u>.

Back To You

I'm fighting for my new day to begin, but I keep getting stopped;

It seems like what's stopping me is a mile high wall made of rocks.

Devil, I'm not going to let your evilness stop me;

You keep turning me the wrong way, but the all mighty god will set me free.

Devil, there's no way you can take over my soul, heart, and mind;

That all belongs to God there's nothing too hard for him to find.

After mom died, I did the dumbest thing and walked away;

I seriously regret that because I put myself in harm's way.

Ever since then, I basically put myself on the devil's destroy roster;

But I pray to God that no weapon formed against me shall prosper.

I know I've done several things wrong and sinned so many times;

The way I've disappointed the Lord I should be charged with a spiritual crime.

It may seem hard to believe but my motivation is true;

I'm going to keep fighting the devil because I'm going to find my way <u>Back To You.</u>

Let Go And Let God

I've been told so many times that I can't help anyone until I help myself;

I do that anyway and all that does is put more pain on myself.

After I walked away I made myself an easy target;

It brought the enemy so close to my soul he could almost get it.

So here I am talking to the Holy Spirit;

Praying daily hoping He can hear it.

Over the years I've kept my pain gathered inside me;

With this pain in me there's no way I could break free.

I've been told several times that I can't do it or I can't make it;

But I know that's the enemy talking;

But because of God, I know how to ignore that and just keep walking.

My dreams have been crushed because of these seizures the enemy has given me;

But as I look up to the sky I know he's saying, "This won't conquer your life just wait and see."

For some reason I think being cut by a knife would give me less pain;

Devil you might as well back off, I have a spiritual umbrella to stop your rain.

I was told a way to get rid of this pain is a counselor but to me it's a fraud;

All I have to do to get rid of my pain is just pray, <u>Let Go And Let God</u>.

Can't Quit

As I give advice to others and watch them heal;

I'm still in strong pain and anger is mostly all I feel.

As I believe my new day is getting closer and closer everyday;

The enemy catches me and turns me the other way.

I can hear him saying "You can't do it just say you're done;

Just take my hand and we can run."

But as I think about what I've been taught by the church and my mother;

I remember this saying, "You only grab God's Hand and no others."

If she was still here I know mom would tell me only God can bring your new day;

All you have to do is take some time and just pray.

I honestly don't know where I'm going with all this pain, anger, and confusion I'm going through;

But I'm 100% sure that to fix this God is the only one I can go to.

When I look to the past and see that I got through this pain I wonder how;

Devil you're done messing with me because I'm over it now.

Saying the devil almost won is something hard to admit;

I refuse to let him win so I know I just <u>Can't Quit</u>.

Hear My Cries

As I think about the pain I go through, I want to ask God to hold me;

I know when He's here the pain will go away and somehow I'd be free.

Momma always told me I'm going to be a strong woman of God, I just want to know when;

Why would He want me if I keep committing sin after sin?

I want to get my breakthrough, but for some reason it just won't come;

I cry out Your name because You're the only one I can get my breakthrough from.

As I look to the sky and scream, "Lord help me!" into the atmosphere;

Nothing seems to come except for a large amount of pain, anger, and fear.

Now that she's with the Lord, momma can no longer quote His word or hold me;

She was the one who prayed and help set me free.

She's gone so I walked away and now I'm trapped again;

It's going to be harder to get out because of all my sins.

I know the word of God, but after her death I stopped obeying it;

Now that I'm going through this pain I'm ashamed I quit.

So here I am fighting to get back with God but I've failed so many tries;

All I can do now is look to the skies, and hope God can <u>Hear My Cries</u>.

Hello Faith Goodbye Fear

When my mother died it became hard to keep positive thoughts in my mind;

I know if she was here she would tell me everything will be just fine.

The devil keeps messing with me, but I'm a strong young woman;

No matter what he does to me I'll be the one that God summons.

With all the pain I go through it's hard not to be scared;

But the Word of God will help me be prepared.

Lord help me to wash all this pain away;

Please shower down because I refuse to let it stay.

The devil and this fear will not take over my mind again.

God will help me because I know He forgave me of all my sins.

To get through this I'm going to need a lot of faith inside me;

I know I can win this battle devil just wait and see.

Momma was right I'm going to be a strong woman of God, stronger than a stone;

With all the faith I'll have one day I'll be called to His throne.

So Lord make me over again so my mind will be clear;

All I have left to say is <u>Hello Faith,</u> <u>Goodbye Fear</u>.

Lesson Not Yet Learned

I hope God doesn't think I'm rushing Him to bring me my new day;

Getting me to the point I can hear anything He has to say.

Rushing Him to make these seizures disappear;

Constantly asking Him to take away all this pain, anger, and fear.

I say Lord forgive me but then I'll go back and do the same old thing;

The way I've disappointed the Lord I need to give Him a promise ring.

To let Him know I'm really trying and my motivation is true;

And that I believe His super natural powers will bring me my breakthrough.

There's something to this confusion because I know God will never give me more than I can bare;

This fear will make me stronger because I'll no longer be one of the ones the devil can scare.

I keep wondering, if I'm back in church, Lord why me?

I'm fighting to get back with You because when I pass I want you to be the one I see.

This pain and confusion level is getting more and more complicated;

All I can do right now is thank the Lord because I'm here so that means I made it.

I'm not going to let this keep me worried and concerned;

Since I'm going through this, I know my <u>Lesson is Not Yet Learned</u>.

Just Know You Can

So many people give up when trouble comes their way;

Just pray to God and ask for the strength to stay.

The enemy comes and hopes to get the best of you;

Just remember what God promised you and know that it is true.

God is a man of the word He spoke;

Once He said it, it won't be revoked.

As long as you listen to everything He tells you to do;

I won't be the only one who receives a breakthrough.

The enemy aims for people who are way too kind;

To win that type of battle you have to think with your soul, heart, and mind.

The enemy will come after you every chance he can get;

Have faith in God and he won't be able to get one little hit.

Never think God gave up on you because He's always at your side;

While He's there, the enemy will just go run and hide.

God will give you a test because He knows you're a strong woman or man;

Just keep faith in God and <u>Just Know You Can</u>.

Never Too Late

After going through that hard time I blamed God and walked away;

I got involved with the wrong people now I don't know what to say.

With all the wrong things I've done, I put myself in a deeper hole;

The pain felt like fire but it wouldn't go out even when I stop, drop, and roll.

Sometimes I sit in bed praying this pain will just disappear;

And that God will shower down and wash away all this fear.

I want to get back with God, but it feels like I'm stuck in a cage;

Hopefully this is just a point in life and soon God will turn the page.

I close my eyes and ask God to send his Holy Spirit;

The enemy gave me a cold heart but with His Holy Spirit I know I can clear it.

God is unique and strong so I know He's truly able;

And if I praise Him the right way I know one day He'll make my soul stable.

It won't be long until my mouth gives Him the ultimate praise;

I just have to wait until God gives me my finals because I know this is a learning phase.

Over time I've doubted myself, but it made no sense to just sit and wait;

Because knowing the God I worship, I know it's <u>Never Too Late</u>.

Take It Away

As I look over my shoulders I see so many people in pain;

The only weather that comes to their lives is a storm of rain.

I can see in their eyes that they're confused and don't know what to do;

They have not yet realized God is the only one who can help them through.

There's others who are so stressed out and suicide is in their mind;

We all know that's not the mindset God made for mankind.

The pain they're going through keeps burning their day;

So I'm begging you Lord please Take It Away.

There's others like me who look at their past and break down into tears;

They keep hoping and praying soon their mind will be clear.

There are other times when I'm in strong physical pain;

But I know soon strength is something I will gain.

God will set many obstacles but through that journey there's a lesson you will learn;

If you want peace from God that's something you have to earn.

God knows when you're in pain so you have to listen to what He has to say;

And after we receive His message just know God will <u>Take It Away</u>.

Forgive To Live

There are so many people who've been hurt so no there's hatred in their hearts

The devil likes thinks like that because now it'll be easier to tear them apart

With hatred in your hearts there's not much a person can do

With hatred and no forgiveness there's not much God can help you through

Sometimes all mean things people have done to you, you have to let it roll off your shoulders

Or the cold heart the enemy is trying to give to you will get much colder

Other times you have to accept it because it'll make you stronger in the long run

Defeating the devils plan will make your day brighter than the sun

Being an unforgiving person is nothing but sinning

Keeping hatred in your heart is bringing the enemy a step closer to winning

Being unforgiving is selfish because there are others who need your survival

With forgiveness your heart and soul will have total revival

If we do like Marvin Sapp says and praise him in advance

I know for sure our forgiving God will give us another chance

You may think you have it all but God has so much more he can give

But to receive it you have to be here so you have to <u>Forgive To Live</u>

Your New Season Shall Come

After going through a hard time people want to give up so fast;

But what you need to do is move to the future and not your past.

If you keep looking back your new day will never begin;

And keeping you in this dark spot will make the devil laugh and grin.

If we give our time to God because we know He's worthy of our praise;

It'll bring us a few steps further from our sinful days.

Because He's Jesus Christ we know He's royalty;

That means we have to stop what we're doing and give him our loyalty.

If we make a promise to God and say "lord I'm coming out;"

He'll help us win our battle because he knows that's not what our life is about.

Giving our loyalty to God can get us so much further than we expected to go;

Our loyalty can help us connect with God in a spiritual flow.

If you believe in God because he's the one we get the Holy Spirit from;

There's no doubt very soon Your New Season Shall Come.

I Want To Believe

There's so many times when I want to lock myself in my room and just cry;

Then hope and pray my faith level will get super high.

With all the pain I am going through, it's hard to keep my faith on the level I need;

Without that faith, it'll be easier for the devil to win, indeed.

There's also times when I want to stop where I am and say "I quit!"

But I know there's another answer to this situation, and that's just not it.

Since the time I was 7 it's been easier for me to be broken hearted;

This random pain won't take over anymore because my breakthrough has already started.

I got a message from God and He said I'll see the devil leave the way he came;

The devil refuses to leave until he takes my faith because that's the reason why he came.

Having the devil take over my mind like this is making it harder to have faith in God's message and my beliefs;

Lord please give me strength so I'll have total release.

Having strength will make it easier for faith to be something I receive;

So Lord please help me, I Want To Believe.

Break Every Chain

There's only so much pain a person can go through in just one day;

Then go looking for advice but God's the only one who truly knows what to say.

As we start to get trapped in this pain, we can't hear his advice that keeps us free;

We begin to get weak and no one helps because our pain is something they can't see.

The weaker we get the devil adds on another chain;

Making it harder to fight through all our pain.

As we begin to get weaker it sometimes pulls us further from Gods' son;

This brings tears to our eyes because we're scared nothing can be done.

Losing faith in God and His son will cause a stronger chain to locked on;

Without faith there's no way that chain will be gone.

With the strong pain we go through it can sometimes cause fear;

Fear is another chain that will bring our eyes a river of tears.

We ALL know God is strong and there's power in His name;

With His almighty power, God will <u>Break Every Chain</u>.

Who He Called Me To Be

The way I was raised, I was taught God is always number one;

And no matter what happens He comes second to none.

After experiencing more things in life, I pulled myself further away;

People tried to warn me but I didn't care about anything they had to say.

As long as I was blending in and looking cool like the other teens;

I didn't care what happened because I was being seen.

Now that I'm older I realize the mistakes I was making;

And now that I'm getting back with God I realize the chances I was taking.

Chances like never hearing Him because I kept doing sin after sin;

I know that will ruin me so I'm never going back there again.

As I look to my past, I see I put myself in a deep, dark hole;

And if I didn't come out there's no way God could rescue my soul.

Even though I'm out I can still be a little naïve;

But no matter what, that mission he gave me I will achieve.

When I finish his mission I'll testify and many people will see;

That even though I went through that dark time I am

<u>Who He Called Me To Be</u>.

With Him Until The End

After going through that hard time I blamed the Lord and stayed away for awhile

The devil finally had my life in his hands so that made him laugh and smile

Once he had my life, he put so much pain, anger, and evilness in my heart

It didn't take long until my life started falling apart

He had me so confused I didn't know where I was going

I thought right was wrong and wrong was right because that's what he kept showing

It took me years to realize what I did was stupid and that I blamed the wrong one

It's not the Lord, but it's the devil I need to get away from.

I remember mom telling me I'm a child of God and will always be protected

Out of all the times I've sinned I'm surprised I'm the one He selected

The one He chose to testify and help others in similar pain

And help them realize to get through this, faith in God is something they need to gain

I'm glad He chose me because now I know one day I'll be able to rejoice

Because I'm stronger now and I made the right choice

I know I've made the Lord frown because of all the times I've sinned

But I've taken my life back and I'm sticking <u>With Him Until The End</u>.

Not My Battle

The devil constantly came after me looking for war;

But I couldn't fight back because my mind, heart, and soul were too sore.

He comes after me in every way he can;

Nightmares at night and seizures so bad it hurts to stand.

He came after me through my heart and weak emotions;

And took it so far by coming after my life devotions.

With all his surprised attacks I don't know which way to go;

I want to run back but something is telling me no.

It's so confusing to know if I should run left or right;

Or if I should be strong and just fight.

It hurts to say that I know if I face him I'd be the one to loose;

That's why it's so confusing to know which way to choose.

I hate the fact that faith in God was something I always lack;

But God is a forgiving man and no matter what, He always has my back.

The devils war intention drives me so crazy he makes my brain rattle;

I've finally realized God has this under control and it's <u>Not My Battle</u>.

Forgive And Forget

It's sad to say that it's common to see me with tears in my eyes;

With all the stress I go through, it's hard to stay strong no matter how hard I try.

Because of all the pain I go through it's hard to keep a smile on my face;

And gaining my strength is a slow processing pace.

I know it's mostly the devil's fault why I keep getting hurt;

He keeps sending things after me to make me feel like dirt.

When I stand up for myself it makes me look like the bad one;

I go looking for advice, but I can't hear the directions from God's son.

I keep wondering why mean things and people constantly come after me;

If I keep believing in God, I know one day I'll see.

The harshness of the things that come after me is so unexpected;

But I have to remember what I was told, that I'll always be protected.

If I keep reacting the way I do, I'll never get to life's next level;

And if I don't move forward, the winner will always be the devil.

That means I have to stop what I'm doing before I do something I'll regret;

And be the bigger person and just Forgive and Forget.

Set Us Free

There are multiple types of pain we can go through in a lifetime;

But to get through it we have to be honest and admit it's the devil's fault and mine.

To teach us a certain lesson God will let the devil do a few little things;

When we get close to learning our lesson our minds will soon ring.

Once we've received the lesson we're supposed to learn;

If we keep following these rules in the future, there are a few things we'll earn.

One thing we'll earn is the honor of hearing God's voice through our own two ears;

And becoming stronger and not sheading so many tears.

Once we become stronger the devil will come after us with a bigger threat;

But with the power of God we will become something he'll never get.

Because we're still on earth there will always be bad times we'll go through;

And we already know God is the only one who knows what to do.

If we stay loyal and dedicated to God soon many people will see;

That from all this pain, anger, and depression God will <u>Set Us Free</u>.

The Better Side

I was raised in church so I know it was wrong, but I kept doing bad

Through all this stress and pain, I couldn't help but to stay mad

The people I thought were my friends didn't help they just walked away from me

Leaving me there alone made it harder to get free

They claim they have my back, but they're never there to catch me when I'm falling

Out of all the people I know there's only one who hears me calling

His name is Jesus Christ and he's my only true friend

He's the one I know for sure will be with me until the end

He gives me chance after chance through all my wrong doings

Because He knows a new beginning is what I'm pursuing

Through all this pain there's barely a smile, mostly a frown

But with all His encouragement and miracles He turns my frowns upside down

Over the years I've realized people have their own point of view so they'll only see what they want to see

So since I'm always upset they'll only see the angry part of me

Jesus has always been with me through my toughest ride

Because like a true friend He always sees The Better Side

My Knight In Shining Armor

Through all the dangers in life, there's only one who can protect me 24/7

It's the man who owns, opens, and protects the holy gates of heaven.

If harm ever came my way He'd be the first to see;

He'd block it because like the Word says, "He'll never leave nor forsake me."

With all the obstacles in life I can't help but to stay concerned;

Because like it or not there is pain around some of these turns.

I've been scared about losing my life because the devil does the most evil things;

But as I think about the power of God, He can stop anything the devil tries to bring.

The demonic plans the devil had for my life made my mind swirl;

I must remember what that bible says and that's that He'll be with me until the very ends of the world.

The devil took my happiness before but that won't be repeated;

There's no doubt that while I'm with the Lord his demonic plans will be defeated.

I know because I'm winning the devil is saying "When I get the chance I'm going to harm her."

That will never happen because God is always at my side, and He

<u>is My Knight in Shining Armor.</u>

Call On You

The devil keeps coming after me trying to bring me down

Removing my smile and replacing it with a frown

Placing so many obstacles in my life trying to pull me further away

Trying to make me think God's no good and pull me closer his way

Devil you might as well back off, I was named after the Jordan River so I'm stronger than you know

If you didn't know, the Jordan River has the world's strongest flow

You've given me seizures for more than 10 years but I'm still standing

No matter how high you try to throw me, God gives me a safe landing

God I need to thank you for waking me up every single day

No matter how many times I've sinned you've allowed me to live another day

I know you have a plan for my life because you promised me a healing

Once you said it I know that's something the devil won't be stealing

Lord thank you for everything you've done for me

Allowing me to live and giving me more things to see

No matter what happens, God is the only one I need to go too

To get through my problems, I know all I have to do is <u>Call On You</u>

Don't Look Back

Because of the obstacles in life, sometimes I get scared and try to run away

I know that's wrong and not of God, but sometimes I think that's the only way

By me running away that would put victory in the devils mind

That will never happen because God says, "She is a child of mine."

As long as I'm a child of God and obey His Word, victory will be in my hands

As long as I believe and have faith in God, I'll always be strong enough to stand

The stronger we get will cause the devil to come after us with a bigger plan

The only one we can depend on is God because he's stronger than man

The devil will first aim for your soul, heart, and mind

Trying to make Jesus and the Holy Spirit something hard for you to find

If we look to the future and thank God for the plan He has for our life

There'll be very few bad things and mostly nice

Thinking about bad things in the past will make us weak and cause faith to be something we lack

So to stay strong and regain our faith we have to remember

<u>Don't Look Back</u>

From The Inside Out

God has sent me many signs but because I wasn't focused on Him I missed each one

Because of fear I had no faith so that made me think I was done

Since I thought I was done I felt like the titanic and thought I was sinking

I have to realize the reason I felt like this is because I always had negative thinking

This negative thinking is causing me to become weak

And this weakness is exactly what the devil seeks

The devil comes after me in every way he can

I guess he expects me to repeat the past because before I've ran

Now that I'm getting back with God running is no longer a choice

Because soon I'll be strong enough to win the war and do nothing but rejoice

So devil get it out of your mind you'll never win and you won't be able to make me scream and shout

God is working on my strength, faith, and he's healing me

<u>From The Inside Out</u>

No Doubt

Even though pain is almost an everyday thing;

As long as we have faith, peace is something our God can bring.

Sometimes our pain comes from our closest ones;

But to get through this we have to believe in God's son.

To try to destroy us, the devil will send pain to us in many different ways;

If we don't have faith and patience in God the pain just stays.

Yes, doing these things are easier said than done;

But if you think about it, you know He's able because He's the one who controls the sun.

So many of us are pushing God away so soon, we won't even be strong enough to stand;

Our God wants to help so we need to grab hold to His outstretched hand.

Helping us through our problems is what our God is all about;

For Him to do this for us, He has to know we believe in Him and have <u>No Doubt</u>.

Defeated

Devil, I bet there's a huge evil smile on your face;

Because you probably think I'm connecting with God at a very slow pace.

If you know I'm finding my way back to God why are you still coming after me?

I guess you don't think I'm strong enough but you just wait and see.

I walked away and you got to me but that will never happen again;

Because I'm only a few steps away from my holy and glorious friend.

God forgave me of all my sins even though they were very wild;

He said it's His blood going through my veins so I'll always be His child.

Devil, you might as well stop trying to remind me of my past and all of my sins;

No matter what you do or say to me there's no way that you'll win.

I know you have evil plans, but I rebuke you and my past won't be repeated;

Even though we haven't went to war, just know you will be <u>Defeated</u>.

Gave My Soul Another Chance

One question, why are you such a forgiving God?

With all the things I do, I look like a Christian fraud.

I've done so many bad things, but you forgave me of my sins;

I could go out and do it over or even worse and you'll still forgive me again.

After I lost my mother, I had nothing but negativity in my mind;

I even blamed You and walked away so why are You still being so kind?

After I walked away, I did wrong and lost faith in your name;

I'm even woman enough to admit that I played into the devil's demonic game.

I hate to say it, but pain is what I mostly go through;

With all of this pain Lord can't You see all I'll do is disappoint You?

You said no but he said yes and I took his side so why won't you give up on me?

A hurtful trader in me is sometimes all I see.

Seeing me like this makes the devil laugh and dance;

But my forgiving God <u>Gave My Soul Another Chance</u>.

Victory

Devil what makes you think you're strong enough to win over me?

God is at my side so defeated is something I'll never be!

You've grabbed hold of my heart and soul like it's a clutch;

But the almighty God set me free that's why I love him so much.

You've done so much to hurt me and try to bring me down;

Thanks to all of your evilness all I could do was frown.

Guess what devil? That weak little girl is no longer here;

This strong woman of God now has no fear.

Now that I'm strong with God and no longer weak;

The devil will have to go after someone else because I no longer have what he seeks.

So all my wrong doing and fears are now history;

Because as long as God's at my side I'll always have <u>Victory</u>!

His Glorious Love

Who or what can I depend on with all these ups and down I keep going through?

I have so many friends and family but there's only a few I can turn to.

I can only turn to a few because some of them are the ones who turned my sunshine into rain;

Even though they're supposed to be the one to bring the umbrella to stop the rain.

Where can I hide to get away from all of this thundering and lighting strikes?

Who can I depend on to give me a solid yes or no instead of all these "I might's."

Now days it's so hard to find a true friend, but it's easy to find someone who will stab you in the back;

Or someone who won't raise your self-esteem but will remind you of what you lack.

I know there's one I can count on even though I've never seen Him or heard His voice;

He's the one who sticks with me even when I make a horrible choice.

Momma taught me He's a man of His word so once He said it I should have no doubt;

Because going back on what He said is not what He's about.

The man I'm talking about is the Almighty King in the heavens above;

I'm glad I remember that to get through this I can always depend on Him, His Word, and <u>His Glorious Love</u>.

A New Beginning

With all the miracles You've done, I've never observed them just took a quick glance;

And with all the wrong doings I've done I have a lot of nerve asking for another chance.

You've given me so many opportunities out of the kindness of Your heart;

But all I did was take advantage of them and tear them apart.

I hate to admit it but I played into the devil's games even though evilness is all he was showing;

After doing such wrong things, I honestly don't know where I was going.

So Lord, I come to you to ask that one day you allow me to see Your face;

Because I'm 100% sure that will put me in a better place.

It's crazy for me to ask such a question because I know the things I've done in God's eyes are forbidden;

Once I thought about it, I had no worries because of the God He is, I've already been forgiven.

All the pain and wrongdoing in my life made my heart and mind blast;

But now I'm a new person and becoming woman of God so all of that is in my past.

I love and worship my God because before I even asked, He forgave me of all my sinning;

And even kept His angels watching over me while giving my life

<u>A New Beginning</u>.

Greatness Within

Sometimes I wonder why people think so low of me

I'm more than just a young woman in pain and soon they'll see

Yes, I admit there's a lot of pain and anger in me but I'm not a hater I'm a lover

I just wish people would do like the saying says and "Never judge a book by its cover"

I know there's one who will never judge me no matter how much anger I have down in my heart

He's the one that will never leave but help me get through it so it won't tear me apart

To be honest with all of this criticism sometimes makes me think I'll never grow up and succeed

But just be a dependent woman and always want and need

With all the targets on my body makes it feel like I'm sinking in

quick-sand,

Feeling this way makes it hard to find my way to the lifestyle God has planned

When I get out of this sand, I'll be stronger from the inside out

I'll let judgement go in one ear and out the other and quit with the doubt

God is blessing me so I need to stop with all of these sins after sins

Because soon he will prove to me and everyone else that I do have <u>Greatness Within</u>

The Highest Praise

God why are you so forgiving to your kids if we keep disappointing you?

We'll break Your rules and keep sinning, but yet You'll still grab our hands and pull us through.

Lord why won't You give up on us and drop our hand?

Leaving us trapped on our knees not being able to stand.

I know since birth You had a plan for our lives and it's already reserved;

But don't You think letting us go and letting us fall is something we deserve?

Since You're our Heavenly Father I know you want to bring peace and happiness to our heart;

But since we keep hurting You, shouldn't You just let us fall part by part?

I've never met anyone like you before;

Because anyone else would go with it and leave us on the floor.

So Lord I'm going to get my life straight and do anything you like;

Go to church as much as possible and worship You with all my might.

Being the type of friend You are there's nothing better I could ask for;

I know with a heart like Yours, you have a wonderful life for me in store.

The kind of God I worship will never let anything bad happen to you not even on your lowest days;

So I'm going to lift my hands in the air, shout hallelujah, and give Him <u>The Highest Praise</u>.

Stronger Than You Know

Dear devil, I'm a woman of God so I'm here to confront you and your demonic plan

Can't you see no matter what you do to me God will always help me to stand?

You've hurt me physically, mentally, and emotionally which made me cry and yell

You even took my mother from me which put my life through hell

You know it's hard for a teenage girl to go through life without her mother?

Especially when she needs that female advice and knows she can't count on any other.

Devil can't you see no matter what you do to me you'll never find me on the ground?

As long as God is at my side you'll never win, and I know you hate the way that sounds

Because of God I'm still standing and defeated is something I'll never be

And because I'm a child of God, victory is in my hands and soon you'll see

You keep trying to bring me down but I've constantly won

You still can't tell you'll never get to me as long as I'm with God and His son

So devil just be smart and turn around and go

Don't let this short girl fool you, I'm <u>Stronger Than You Know</u>

Hear Your Voice

I know I'm going through all of this pain because the devil hates that I'm finally trying to get my life together;

I can't stay like this, keep sinning, and go through this pain forever.

Every time I think I'm getting closer something happens and fills my body up with nothing but madness;

Or get put through so much emotional pain my heart gets filled with nothing but sadness.

I hate that I can't keep a smile on my face for more than a day;

Still not strong enough to pay no attention to the mean things others have to say.

Many things can bring my emotions so far down;

One mean thing can make me explode with anger and put my smile 6ft under the ground.

At times I'm so strong I'm the one people come to when they're hurt and crying;

Other times I'm so hurt I want to give up on all the things I'm trying.

Sometimes by the looks of it, it seems like I'm not going to get anywhere;

With all this anger it seems like I don't belong anywhere.

Going through all this pain makes it seem like happiness is no longer a choice;

But I know to get through this all I need to do is <u>Hear Your Voice</u>.

A Slower Pace

Someone like me is often not in the right state of mind

We're constantly getting hurt for being too kind

With the amount of times I've been hurt I can say it's way more than a few

Going through all that pain gave me a negative point of view

Even though I'm going through a hard time I'm too concerned about how others

feel

When I know I need to worry about myself because my soul is something the devil

is trying to steal

My mom always taught me that I need to worry about myself before I can worry

about others

No matter how close we are even if it's her, daddy or my brothers

I know God is the only way to go so I pray everyday

I'm not making any progress because I didn't listen to what my mom had to say

Since I'm so concerned about my loved ones connecting with God and putting

their lives in a better place

I never made time for God and myself so I'm connecting with Him at

<u>A Slower Pace</u>

Lord Why Me

Sometimes with all this pain I go through I can only say, "Lord Why Me?"

I know I messed up by walking away from You

But because I'm finding my way back, the devil's making smiling something hard for me to do

Every time I think I'm getting spiritually closer to improve all the things I lack

Somehow the enemy catches me and pulls me further back

Once again all I can say is "Lord Why Me?"

I hate to say I've been sick for most of my life so far

I'm a young woman and I can't do like others so it feels like I'm trapped behind bars

At the moment, I can't hear Your voice, but I was told you promised me a healing

I started gaining faith which the Devil hates, so more often he started stealing

You already know what's coming next so........"Lord Why Me?"

Because I had faith more and more pain started to come

I went searching for years but I didn't know where I could get happiness from

After I lost faith all I could do was constantly cry rivers of tears

Since I lost faith all I did was gain more fears

"Lord Why Me?"

I'm so concerned about my loved ones and all their pain

I'm holding myself back from that faith I need to gain

How am I being so naive that I'm playing into the devil's game

I know if I was smart enough to walk away my breakthrough would've already came

"<u>Lord Why Me</u>?"

I don't know why but the devil keeps trying to take my family away

First my mom from cancer, now my dad, but I rebuke that and he's going to stay

Mom always taught me praying is the main thing I need to do

I pray every night but it seems like nothing is new

So "<u>Lord Why Me</u>?"

Come To An Ending

With all the wrong doings I've done I put my life in the devil's hand

Since he had control over my life he made it hard for me to stand

It took me a year to realize I was disappointing the Lord and I needed to change my ways my

And if I kept doing what I was doing the devil wins and the pain would stay

But if I don't change, my life, heart, and soul will stay in a horrible place;

That means when my time comes I'll would never see the Lord's face.

The devil has given me seizures for more than 11 years

That made it hard to be independent so that made me constantly shed tears

Shedding all those tears made me angry which put me through more pain

The anger made it harder for me to love because over my heart I had a big black stain

Because of all this anger I became a hater and not a lover

With the sinning I did, I made my soul cold and always needed a cover

I don't know what I did but destruction to my life is what the devil keeps sending

But I know with the power of God, this pain and these seizures will <u>Come To An Ending</u>

Too Scared To Know

I can't even begin to describe all the things the devil has put me through;

While going through it I never knew the right one to turn to.

There's my dad, my brothers, and other family members but I never knew which one;

I always wanted to turn to God, but I could never hear His voice or His son.

I know deep down inside I'm a spiritually strong young woman;

But because I'm so lost, I don't know when I'll be summoned.

I've went left and right but I still never went in the right direction;

Every time I think I'm getting closer, I feel nothing but rejection.

I'm trying to get my life together, but it feels impossible;

I know I have to keep faith because the power of God is unstoppable.

I just wish I was strong enough to keep my heart and soul stable;

I know soon I'll get there because God and His son are more than able.

Sometimes I wonder with this lifestyle where am I going to go;

I wonder how am I going to get there but I'm just <u>Too Scared To Know.</u>

My Season

One day I'm strong and the next day I'm weak so the devil got to my mind;

Once he has it in his hand he makes it hard for me to find.

Without my mind, it's impossible for me to make the right decisions;

And making the wrong ones will get me in multiple collisions.

Making the wrong choices will get me in so much trouble;

Getting put in trouble, all that drama will just make all this pain double.

Devil why are you coming after me? What did I ever do to you?

You've taken some loved ones and diagnosed me with epilepsy so that's a lot of pain you've put me through.

I pray a lot so God rained on me so much it caused a flood;

I rebuke the fact that you can get to me anymore because I plead the blood.

I let the Devil into my life because of my sinful days;

But soon I'll be strong enough to give God all my praise.

I know God is allowing me to go through these things for a reason;

I guess He's giving me a testimony because soon it'll be <u>My Season.</u>

Hold On Tight

Why does it seem like this pain is getting worst and worst?

If things keep going the way they are, soon my heart will just burst.

I keep losing so many people especially the ones so important to me;

When I was feeling down, they gave me the advice that helped me see.

People keep telling me, "Hold your head up and soon you'll get stronger;"

But with all this pain I don't know if I can make it much longer.

With all this heavy pain it's weighing me to the ground;

Seems like no one understands me, so will I ever be found?

Lord I know You see me so please do something to get me back on my feet;

I know You believe in me and there's an expectation You want me to meet.

How can I ever get to that point if I keep losing faith in Your Word;

Running away from my problems because it feels like I'm not being heard.

I remember mom teaching me always have faith in God's Word no matter how low you feel;

Because someone's faith in his word is one of the main things the Devil tries to steal;

You're a child of God and He's strong so He will protect you with all His might;

All you have to do is be strong, have faith, and <u>Hold On Tight</u>.

The Fighter Inside

I admit, The devil got to me and put my life through hell

I tried to hide all of this pain but somehow, people could still tell

Some people care enough to stop and ask "Are you okay?"

While others keep walking, laugh, and have nothing to say

When I feel down and out, I feel nothing but fear

And when I feel down and out, I lock myself in my room and shed tears

When people see me like this, they think I'm just one weak little girl

They think because I'm emotional there's nothing I can do in this world

Going through all this makes it seem like my life is being put on a rough ride

Even though it seems like everyone lost faith in me I know there's still one at my side

He's the spirit in the heavens who gets all the glory

The only one out there who has faith in my story

I've been put through a lot but by his stripes I am healed

One day I'll have to go to war and he'll be my shield

When that time comes, if I want to win, there's rules he made that I must abide

Then the devil and everyone else will see <u>The Fighter Inside</u>

Evicted

Devil I have a message for you so open both of your ears

Just know soon I'll have happiness and no fears

You came in my life and you killed, stole, and destroyed

I know one day I'll be working for God so soon I'll be employed

Once I'm working under his name, you'll never be able to get to me again

No matter how much wrong I've done or how many times I've sinned

You stole my life's plans and destroyed my highest dream

Leaving me in so much pain and making me feel like I always want to scream

Once you came in my life you got to my soul, heart, and mind and got the best of me

Now that I'm finding my way back to God you will not get the rest of me

So, devil, I'm not that same little girl that you almost beat

Because I'm getting closer to God so I'm no longer that weak

I have one more thing to say, so Devil from this point on my soul, heart, and mind are strongly restricted

So, go pack your bags and leave because devil from my life you're officially Evicted.

All Be Gone

It's so crazy how sometimes I will go through so much pain in just one day

With it coming by surprise I never have anything to say

Because I'm speechless I can't do anything but lay down and shed so many tears

And when this happens, I'm not as strong so the devil can see all my fears

Seeing me like this makes the devil happy because that's exactly what he seeks

By me shedding so many tears I admit it makes me very weak

I use to have a woman who made me strong and helped me through all of this pain

Now that she's gone strength is not so easy for me to gain

That woman I knew was a woman of God and also my mother

Since she's not here all I have is my friends, father, and brothers

With these seizures, crushed dreams, and mom gone sometimes I ask the Lord why me

Please tell and show me what I did wrong I need to see

Because I sinned and walked away from him I can't hear his voice

But I have no one to blame but myself since that was my choice

So lord I apologize that I left you all alone

And Lord please forgive me and soon <u>All Be Gone</u>

My 7th Day

How can such a short body like mine carry so much pain?

With all the up and down weather in my life it feels like it's mostly rain.

I've done so much wrong in the past so my sin is something I'll try address;

But the more I try to fix it and do right the more I stress.

These are some of the main reason I wish I could hear God through my own two ears;

There's no way that can happen if the devil keeps winning and conquering over me with fears.

If I'm too scared to make the next move, how will I ever be strong enough to fight?

And not making that next move, makes victory impossible to be in sight.

Soon I won't be so weak, and the enemy will no longer get to my mind;

Because I'm a winner and my way back to God is something, I'm too eager to find.

It took the Lord 6 days to create the world and on the last day He stopped to rest;

Only He can do such things without any pain or stress because He's known as the best.

So Lord I come to You to give You all this hurt and hear what You have to say;

I know it's because of You that I'm half way there and soon it'll be <u>My 7th Day</u>.

I'm Coming Out

I hate to say this, but the devil got to me but I started with a great beginning

Once momma left I walked away, lost faith, and started sinning

After sinning so much I ended up putting my life into the wrong hand

Once I lost control over it, it was impossible to stay on my own feet and just stand

I know walking away from the Lord is the dumbest thing I could ever do

Now that I'm going through so much hurt and stress I don't know who else to turn to

Because of the way I treated Him I wouldn't blame him if He said, "No, now turn around."

But I'm glad that's not how the Lord is so I know soon my soul will be found

When my soul is found I know the Lord will teach me how to live my life the right way

And soon I'll be able to hear through my own two ears what He has to say

Once I get to that level I won't be so weak anymore

Then I won't have to depend on others because my heart won't be so sore

So Devil back off and that plan you have is not what my life is about

I'm gaining more faith in God's Word and from all this wrong <u>I'm Coming Out</u>

The Reflection Of God's Child

Lord with all this sinning and all my wrong doings why are You still at my side?

I even went overboard and blamed You for the reason my mother died.

After I walked away the enemy got to me and gave me so many fears;

I was always so mad and stressed so I'd shed many tears.

I walked away for years so my way back to God was something I thought I'd never see;

So Lord with all this negativity on my mind why won't You give up on me?

Lord how can you have so much faith in me when I'm full of doubt?

Once I get mad, I can never keep victory and deliverance in my mind even when that's something I always think about.

Even though I keep making horrible choice after choice;

God didn't give up on me and still is soon allowing me to hear His voice.

I think I finally know why He won't give up on me, I'm his daughter!

Hopefully He's saying, "Soon she'll learn the lessons that I've taught her."

Lord I thank You for not giving up on me, even though my sinful choices were wild;

Now I know no matter what I do if I look in the mirror I will ALWAYS see <u>The Reflection of God's Child.</u>

Impossible For You To Win

Hurt and stress is something I constantly go through

But to get rid of this there's only one I can go to

He's the man who created me and it's His blood flowing through my veins

He's so strong and powerful, He's the only one who can wipe away this type of pain

I admit, since I walked away I'm not as strong as I use to be

It won't be like this forever devil, you just wait and see

You may not believe it but my way back to God is my number one goal

So devil no matter what you do to me, God will be the one with my soul

I know it amuses you to put me through so much that my smiles are replaced with frowns

But you should know by now that I'm getting stronger, and you can't keep me on the ground

The Lord Jesus Christ is not just my father He's my true friend

That means I'll never be alone because He'll be at my side until the end

That's why I worship Him!! He won't stop forgiving me even when I disobey His word and sin

Can't you see with the plan the Lord has for my life, Satan it's <u>Impossible For You To Win</u>

I'm Taking My Life Back

I'm ashamed I got involved with the wrong people and started doing the wrong things

I knew what I was doing was not of God and the amount of evil to my life it brings

I didn't stop because I wanted to look cool and blend in with the other teens

By me doing all of that I was giving my life to the devil and that's all that means

Because I kept doing wrong I put my life into the devil's hands

Since he had control over my life he kept me on my knees and made it hard for me to stand

Me being on my knees means I wasn't strong enough to get up and walk away

Therefore I kept reliving the same things day after day

Living the same thing over and over was scary and kept me so concerned

Being worried 24/7 made it hard for my lesson to be learned

I thank the Lord for giving me back my strength and putting me back on my feet

Re-teaching me the lesson I ignored in the past and helping me reach the every expectations He wants me to meet

So Lord I come to You to apologize for the amount of belief and faith that I lack;

Lord please forgive me and Devil expect my arrival because I'm

<u>Taking My Life Back</u>

His Next Move

Sometimes I wonder how I can be a child of God if it's hard for me to believe?

Thinking I'm not strong enough to complete the mission He wants me to achieve.

I was raised in church, so I know what the Lord is about;

I know He's a man of His word so I don't understand why I have doubt.

One minute I think I'm strong and I know I can do it;

The next minute I'm too weak and need someone to help me through it.

God is the only one who can get me in my right state of mind;

Because He's more powerful than all of mankind.

With all that power there's so many miracles He can work;

He's the one who can deliver us from all this hurt.

I'm trying to give my life back to God even though I know I'm not complete;

I'm working on getting myself to the level the Lord needs me to meet.

To get to that level there's a lot I need to prove;

So I pray now that healing and making me whole will be

<u>His Next Move</u>.

It Shall Be Done

One thing we should all know is that there's nothing God can't do

He's the one who created the universe so He can definitely break us through.

He's the miracle worker and the leader of mankind;

The one who helps us get to things that are usually impossible to find.

That man gave up His life for us and was pinned to a cross;

The one who came back stronger and there's not a war He has ever lost.

If it wasn't for Him and His power, none of us would be here;

He's the one who grabbed and delivered us from fear.

God is like no other, He's a very unique man;

He can do things no human being can.

If God makes you a promise just know it will come to pass;

And any miracle He's performed will always last.

The Devil will try to mess with you, but when he sees God he'll run

Even though it may take some time, when God gives you His word,

<u>It Shall Be Done</u>

The Only One There

I don't understand how I have so many people in my life but yet I feel alone

Going through so much pain makes it feel like I bashed my foot against a stone

They claim they love me but in a quick second they'll leave my side

Especially the ones who told me they'll be there with me even on my roughest ride

Why make me a serious promise you know you won't keep

You know a ride or die friend is something everyone will seek

My so-called loved ones are basically leaving me one by one

But I know there's one I can go to and that's Gods almighty son

He's the one who will come to me so I can use his shoulder to cry

He'll let me shed a few tears then build me back up to help me fly

He won't let me sit there depressed feeling down and out

He needs to be around positive feelings because negativity is not what he's about

Jesus has a big heart, so I know he cares

It a shame that sometimes I feel like he's <u>The Only One There</u>

In The Right Direction

I'm not afraid to admit that I've sinned too many times and done so much wrong

I know if I would've stopped what I was doing and stayed with God I could've stayed strong

I don't know why but after losing my mom, believing was something hard for me to do

Especially with all this constant pain I keep going through

I've been told several times that God has a breakthrough waiting for me and soon I'll receive it

It's just that It seems like this pain Is getting worse so It's kind of hard to believe It

Lord I don't know why I have lack of faith since I know who You are

You're the only one I know who can deliver me and take me so far

I want to come back to you but no matter where I go, I end up turning the wrong way

With it being hard for me to believe sometimes I want to quit, stop where I am and just stay

Lord I promise you I'm working on my faith and belief so I can give you my life's devotion

I know that promise of a breakthrough and healing Is In motion

So, Lord I come to You and ask that You bless me with strength to fight through all this constant rejection

And please give me Your hand and guide me <u>In The Right Direction</u>

I'll No Longer Be The Same

Sometimes I constantly have negativity in my mind

Thinking my way back to the Lord is something I'll never find

I don't know why I think like this since I was raised by a minister and choir director

Maybe it's because she's gone so Lord, I ask that You protect her

Lord can You please explain to me why I think and feel this way?

Help me realize it won't be like this every day

I know if I don't start thinking positive in the end the Devil could be the one with my soul

Since day one that's something the Devil always wanted, but I'm going to make sure he doesn't reach his goal

With all the things I go through I can't afford to be a negative thinking human being

My negative thinking is causing bad things to be all I'm experiencing and seeing

Seizures, loss of loved ones, physical and emotional pain

I'm waiting for the sun to shine but over my life but I keep receiving a storm of rain

So Lord I come to You on bended knees asking You to change me

Please help me believe that there's so much more I can be

Lord help me get to that point where I can be anywhere and still feel Your spirit

I ask that You get me to that stage where I can be around so much negativity and if You're talking, I can still hear it

When the Lord gets me to these levels Devil just know I'll be strong enough to never again play into your evil demonic game

When I get there I'll be that STRONG woman of God therefore,

<u>I'll No Longer Be The Same</u>

The Praise He Deserves

It's a shame how God does so much for us and some of us don't even say thank you

We just sit there receive his blessings and act like there's nothing we supposed to do

I know if it wasn't for the lord my God, I'd still be in such a wrong state of mind

I'd still cut myself, think of suicide, and still hate man kind

The Lord has always been at my side and has kept me from falling

He's helped me get through all this hurt so I can receive and be successful in my calling

If it's what's for my almighty God I wouldn't be here, I'd be dead

Because of these seizures I could die if I ever hit my head

Over the years of having seizures I've had big ones and busted my head so many times but I'm still here today

I've been in and out of hospitals and the doctors will tell my parents she's fine, be careful and take your meds'; and that's all they have to say

I've left the lord so many times, but he would never leave my side

I know if I'm ever lost and stranded, I can count on God for a ride

The Lord has given people messages to give me because right now I can't hear him through my own two ears

The messages are usually so strong and just how I feel so I end up in tears

I honestly don't know where I'd be without my heavenly father above

There's nothing I would be able to do or be if it wasn't for his strong love

Our calling, blessing, and miracles that the Lord has for us is already reserved

Before we can receive those things we need to thank the Lord by looking up, lifting our hands and giving God <u>The Praise He Deserves</u>

Not Time For My Ending

There's just so much extreme pain I keep going through;

There's people in my life who have their own so I don't know who to turn too.

These seizures and random black outs are bringing me down;

But I can't keep letting this happen because it's replacing my smile with a frown.

Constantly frowning and crying will make the enemy think he's winning;

Devil just know the Lord has a plan for my life and this is only the beginning.

Soon I'll be that strong woman the lord created me to be;

The delivered woman who can receive God's message through her own 2 ears and soon everyone will see.

God's plan will make me less sensitive and much stronger;

That mean this hurt and these seizures won't be in my life much longer.

This pain and negativity had had me placed on the ground;

Even though at the moment I'm not where I need to be with the Lord I know my soul will be found.

The Lord my God is my Heavenly Father so I know I'll always have His hand;

Therefore if I ever get placed on the ground again all I have to do is pray, stretch out my arm and He'll help me stand.

When I get my breakthrough I can't wait to prove everyone wrong who counted me as disabled;

I've told them I can do anything they can do and I'm more than able.

So devil all that negativity and evilness my way you keep sending;

I have bad news for you, the Lord has barely started so it's

<u>Not Time For My Ending.</u>

Closer Than You Know

I've been through so much and I don't know where or how to begin my story

What I do know is that I wouldn't be here if it wasn't for the Lord's Almighty Glory

I've been knocked down so many times I gave up and just stayed on the ground

But as I think about the goodness of Jesus, I know He can make me stronger and turn my life around

I know there's others who are so stressed because the pain they keep going through

And probably confused like me on who they can trust and turn too

I know sometimes it's hard to keep faith and constantly believe

One thing we all know is that God is the strongest of all and there's nothing to hard for him to achieve

With the strength of our Lord, there's no way He can't stop this pain

He's so powerful He can make faith and strength something easy for us to regain

The Lord will never leave our side so I know we'll always have a shoulder to cry on

After sheading those tears and pouring our heart out to the Lord it won't be long until the rain is gone

So Devil you might as well stop now because there's no way you'll win

If we're dedicated, God will still guide us to victory even when we sin

Right now it may seem like mostly negative things are happening to you

Just lift your hands, look to the heaven, and tell God you have faith that will help you through

Keep the faith of getting stronger and connecting with God's spiritual flow

Because your healing, strength, victory, and deliverance is

<u>Closer Than You Know</u>

Where I Truly Belong

When I lost my mother I gave my life to the wrong one and turned the wrong way;

After making that huge mistake it seemed like I was going through pain everyday.

Constantly going through pain made me angry so I decided to keep doing wrong;

I had to realize if I kept disobeying the Word of God I won't be here too long.

While doing all this wrong I thought I was cool and protecting my rep;

I soon realized what I was doing was simply sending myself to hell step by step.

In high school I wanted to be cool and blend in with the other teens;

Turning my back on God and playing into the devil's game is basically all that means.

It took me years to realize I was wrong and that I needed to turn my life back in the right direction;

I just thought if I did I'll look lame and receive so much rejection.

If I want to turn my life the right way I need to be able to feel God's spirit;

And when He's sending me a message, I'm the one who needs to be able to hear it.

Now I'm working on getting my life together and putting everything in God's hands;

Learning to have faith in His word because when we fall He's the only one who picks us up helping us to stand.

I go to church as much as possible and now sometimes I can feel His spiritual flow;

I think I'm getting my life together heading the way the Lord wants me to go.

I know if I stay in my right state of mind, soon I'll be strong;

I finally realize the church and God's arms is <u>Where I Truly Belong.</u>

Find My Way

I was raised in church so I'm ashamed to say I'm not in the right spiritual place I need to be

I should be at the place where I can turn anywhere, and victory would be the main thing I see

My mom was a minister so she's the one who taught me most of the things I know

She taught me that to live a better life and living the right way God is the only way to go

With all of this stress and pain I go through sometimes I just want to look up and say, "Lord I quit!"

But as I think about it there's so many things I need to say to my king and that's just not it

Back in the day I was able to speak that heavenly language that only God understood what I was saying

Once I started getting older I got involved with the wrong people and it was His Word that I started disobeying

I'm mature enough to admit I've done a lot of crazy things that I truly regret

Some were so crazy they're unfortunately almost impossible to forget

I know I'm not in my right state of mind because it's full of negativity and doubt

Devil you need to back off because that's not what my life is about

Even though I left His side, God never left mine since He has a plan for me

I may not be very strong right now, but I will get there devil you just wait and see

I'm strong enough to live and get through life day by day

So Lord I come to You on bended knees surrendering myself asking You to help me <u>Find My Way</u>

Already Defeated

It's so hard to convince myself and others that I'm a strong woman if I'm always shedding tears

Even harder to keep a smile on my face if I have so many fears

With all this pain I don't think I'm heading in the right direction

Because of the ways I've went in the past I received constant rejection

I refuse to quit and give up because I'm taking my life back

So Lord, I ask that You forgive and cleanse me even though faith was something I lack

My King is a man of His Word so I know I'll be healed, and my soul will be found

Then I won't have to worry about always being pushed to the ground

Soon I'll be that strong woman the Lord called me to be

I'll be able to complete my mission and finally be free

I'm going to replace this frown by putting a smile on my face

Once I do this everybody will see I'm in a better place

Because of who God is and things He can and will do, my life is a full miracle flood

The best way to thank Him is praising and worshipping His blood

The Lord has done so much for me and my loved ones, so He deserves ALL the glory

When I get in the right place, I'll have a wonderful testimony about my life's story

Victory is already in my hands, so those negative days won't be repeated

So devil just know there's no way you can win because you're

<u>Already Defeated!</u>

It Is So!

Sometimes I just don't know where I'm going with all of this stress

Constantly running into the devil's evil plans and mess

Always scared of receiving more pain and rejection

The Lord tells me to go one way and I end up in the opposite direction

I get knocked to my knees with no strength to get up and run

Seems like I see more storms of rain than the brightness of the sun

I get emotional and let the harsh things people say get the best of me

Being so mad and depressed makes happiness something hard for me to see

I know the only way to get through this is praising Him and hearing His voice

Once I do, I'll be able to fight through negativity and finally rejoice

When I get my strength, I'll be able to fulfill my mission and become that strong woman He created me to be

From all of this sinning, and wrongdoing, I'll be strong enough to walk away and be free

Even with this pain I know somewhere inside me I have a wonderful praise

One so strong I know the Lord will help me forget about these painful days

The Lord has stayed at my side even when I left His, so I know he'll never go

Since He's still with me and promised me deliverance and healing

I know It Is So!

In Your Hands

Will all these things going on in my life I honestly don't know where to start;

By the way things are going sometimes it feels like my life is falling apart.

Constantly in the doctor's office because of these seizures;

Times like this is why I wish Momma was here, but she's in a better place so only God can see her.

Going through things like this is hard especially since I can't hear His voice;

I know God has a plan for my life, but because I can't hear Him I don't know if I've been making the right choice.

I feel like I'm on my own so I'm trying to get strong and go through this alone, but I know that's not right;

I've been told several times by many people that God has this under control so it's not my battle to fight.

I'm doing what I can because it seems like things are getting worst or just staying the same;

Because I'm trying to fight God's battle I know I'm playing into the devil's demonic game.

With all this negativity in my life it's hard for me to keep a positive mind;

Thinking about it so much is causing me to be sad, mean, and angry instead of happy, nice, and kind.

I refuse to let this stress, hurt, and pain take over my life any longer;

Soon all of that will not be able to knock me down because I'll be stronger.

Devil I tell you right now you're done messing with me and playing me like I'm a toy;

God is changing me, renewing my life, and filling it with joy.

Lord I ask that You help me find who I truly am and keep me on my feet to stand;

I know You are more than able so I place all of this stress, hurt, and pain

<u>In Your Hands.</u>

Am I Being Heard

I don't know where to begin to describe all this stress and hurt

I try to clean my soul, heart, and mind but it seems like it's still covered in negativity dirt

I look around and I see people's lives getting better in some type of way

But for me it seems like it's staying the same or getting worst maybe every other day

I'm ashamed to say I'm not in my right state of mind so Lord I don't think I can do this much longer

I honestly don't know where I'm going to end if I don't get stronger

I can't keep living this life if nothing is ever going to change

Living the same things over and over will just make my life strange

You're the creator of the universe so I know there's nothing You can't do

So Lord I ask that You grab my hand and pull me through

Are all of these things happening to me because my faith level is in the wrong place?

Or is it just that the things I want and need are something I need to chase?

The lack of faith is not intended, it's just hard dealing with these horrible things

Being in this situation it is hard fighting through what the devil brings

Lord why can't I be strong enough to stay on my own two feet to stand?

Why do I keep having to ask people for help by giving me their hand?

I read my scriptures, say my prayers, and go to church just about every Sunday to receive you word

I know you have to take care of the universe but even when I pray it seems like nothing's happening so Lord I just wonder Am I Being Heard?

I'm More Than Able

Going through the things I have to deal with is more than just stressing

It has had me think about suicide so it made my life depressing

It's made me feel so weak and filled my heart and soul with doubt

Feeling so weak and defeated has also filled me with anger which makes me want to scream and shout

Sometimes it feels like no one sees me, they just see these seizures

With me feeling alone I know the devil's laughing saying, "Haha nobody sees her."

So Lord I come to You on bended knees asking You to shower down washing away all of my fears

Please rain on me and make me strong so I'll no longer shed so many tears.

Since I'm trying to get my life together and fulfill my duties why did all this happen to me?

I go to church just about every Sunday and receive your word but nothing new seems to be

Lord I ask that You make me strong so I can finally fight and deal with these unheavenly things

Make me so strong that I can handle ANYTHING the devil tries to bring

I can't keep being that woman he can easily knock down and walk on

I want to be so strong where I can walk right pass him and shout, "That weak little girl is gone!"

I'm no longer a little girl so I need to be strong enough where I can be independent since I'm counted as grown

I need to be at the level of faith where I know when my time comes I'll be called to the thrown

So Lord I ask that You help me get to the point where my faith, my soul, heart, and mind stay stable

Help me keep faith in Your promise and believe in myself that I'm <u>More Than Able</u>

I Speak Life

In my life it seems like I get more bad news than good;

Some of my family's health are in the wrong place so they doubt we'll heal but I know we would.

We admit some of the things we go through is so hard and stressful that we want to say we're done;

But we know by doing such a thing we'll be putting our lives in hands that don't belong to God's son.

Putting our lives in those hands means we're turning ourselves in the wrong direction;

How can we live our lives right if we only receive rejection?

Those hands would control our lives and have us doing the wrong things;

By doing that, we'll never collect the wonderful gifts in our lives that the Lord tries to bring.

I know He promised me a healing and a breakthrough but sometimes it feels like this pain will never go;

Constantly feeling this way makes it impossible for me to feel or connect with God's spiritual flow.

I may not be in the right place with God but that doesn't make me a weak woman;

No matter what, I have a calling for my life so soon I'll be the on He'll summon.

I can't keep letting this hurt take over my mind and weakening my heart;

If I do that I'm allowing the enemy to enter my life part by part.

I'm not going to let this conquer me so I lift my hands and plead the blood;

The Lord is great and worthy to be praised so I know He'll fill my life with a spiritual flood.

God is at my side so I know He'll help me and my loved ones fulfill our calling;

And help us stay on our feet and keep us from falling.

The pain hurts so bad I think it's worst than being cut by a knife;

But Satan I rebuke you and death so over my loved one and myself I Speak Life.

Thank You

I honestly don't know where to begin to describe all of this pain

It hurts so much that it makes me mad so sometimes I think over my heart there's a big black stain

How could I ever get my life together and do right by God if I have a stained heart

Always worrying and thinking this will cause my life to slowly fall apart

I admit, with this negative thinking I've made several wrong connections

Because of that I've turned myself in many wrong directions

With all the wrong things I've thought, said, and done I don't see how I'm still here today

I guess that means He has a plan for my life and expects me to hear what He has to say

Lord with all this wrong doing why won't You walk away and give up on me

I've failed You because it's been over 20 years and I'm still not where You wanted me to be

These seizures aren't getting any better so it seems like I'm a step away from saying "I'm done."

By me feeling this way I'm pulling myself further away from God's son

From this point I have no clue where I'm going to go

Feeling like this there's no way I can connect with God's spiritual flow

I don't see how I have a calling for my life if I keep letting Him down

God is a wonderful and victorious so He deserves to smile and not frown

God is the type of man that when He gives you His word He won't take it back

He'll still keep it even if faith in His Word is something you lack

So Lord I ask for Your forgiveness from all these years of doubt even though there's so much You've pulled me through

I come to You on bended knees with my hands stretched to the heavens, "Lord I just want to <u>Thank You</u>"

Make Me Stronger

Sometimes when I go to church my pastor will preach about the exact things I'm going through

But when God tells her to stop and lay hands on someone I'm never the one she goes to

Other times she preaches about the exact way I'm thinking or feeling

And again when God tells her to stop and lay hands on someone it's never for me and my healing

Lord if You have her preaching about the things I go through why won't You ever have her pray for me?

Since she preaches about the things I think and feel how come I'm someone she never sees ?

With me feeling so alone, Lord how can I ever reach my calling?

Feeling like this, how can I be strong enough to keep myself from falling?

I know it's not true but with all of this hurt I go through sometimes it feels like you don't care

And that you're allowing me to go through more than I can bare

Feeling so weak makes me look like a target that can easily be defeated

So Lord I need Your help because I'm not strong enough to handle these days being repeated

I've been worshipping You since I was in my mother's belly

That's why I don't know why so much hurt is in my life so Lord please tell me

I honestly don't know how much longer I can keep feeling down and out

Going through this is just so hard that sometimes I want to stop what I'm doing and just scream and shout

You've pulled me over many mountains and seen me through many trials but I don't think I can deal with this hurt any longer

I come to You pouring out a river of tears asking You to help me stay on my feet and <u>Make Me Stronger</u>

All For My Good

At this point in life things seem to get more complicated just about every other day

Being in my situation this complication hurts and it causes me to always go the wrong way

Going through all of this hurt sometimes makes it hard to have faith and believe

Feeling this way makes it seem like happiness and positivity is impossible to receive

Lord I just want to know since I'm trying to get my life together why is all of this happening to me

If I keep feeling so down and out, how can I ever become that strong woman You created me to be

Having a mindset like this there's no way possible I can do right by You

Most of the time I go to the wrong person thinking they can help me through

I'm trying to get myself to start walking in the right direction and live my life for Jesus

I know that's the right thing to do because He's the only one who truly sees us

I don't know if this hurt is a trip to victory or if it's the devil playing a game

I want to be so strong where I can easily look at the devil and say, "from this point on I'll never be the same."

I can't keep being this woman who can constantly get negativity put in her mind

If I stay like this my way back to God will be impossible for me to find

Lord please tell me what did I do that was so wrong that caused me to get put through all of this hurt

This pain is so bad that it made me depressed to the point that I felt like dirt

You're my heavenly father and I know you care so soon I'm going to get that place where I can hear you say "I knew you could"

That'll mean I reached my calling therefore this journey through this pain turned out to be <u>All For My Good</u>

Made in the USA
Columbia, SC
10 July 2019